Email To Cleveland

poems by

Elaine Heveron

Plain View Press
P. O. 42255
Austin, TX 78704

plainviewpress.net
sb@plainviewpress.net
1-512-441-2452

Copyright Elaine Heveron, 2007. All rights reserved.
ISBN: 978-1-891386-84-8
Library of Congress Number: 2007931093

Cover artwork by April Laragy "Where You End I Begin" watercolor on paper http://www.aprillaragy.com

Contents

Introduction	9

Where I'm From 11

I'll Never Dance With My Father	13
Where I'm From	14
Email To Cleveland	16
Another Business Trip	17
Valentine	18
This Time	19
My Kin	20
Leaves Leaving Summer	21
Birthday Dream In Rome	22
Amnesty Email	23
Spaces	23
C & D Lawn No More	25
Maybe They Call It Spring?	26
The Crying Room	28
I Wish You'd Met My Dad	29
The Airplane Shirt	30
Broken Leg	32
After the Move	33
Nearly Drowned	34
Onion Soup	36
My Father's Car	37
KJ2P 88	38
A Buddhist Waits For Easter	39
The Pair	40
Omega Massage	41
Coyote Man	42
How It Is To Be Retired	43
You Can't File a River Away	44
Peter	45
Bernie	46
Going Deaf	47
A Moment Remembered At Corpus Christi	48
Dear Dad	49
Autumn Without You	50

You Go Girl   51

Carol's Tights	53
Snapshot For a Birth Mother	54
Transformations	56
Garage Sale Item #1	61
Flying Home From Rome	62
Blank Canvas	63
Garage Sale Item #2	64
Not Her Boyfriend	65
Dance Recital – Tap I	66
Earrings	67
Betsy	68
I've Got Your Eyes Today	69
Black Currant Tea	70
Native American Dental Assistant	72
Sister	73
Muriel's Place	74
Seal and Barry	76
Sixtieth Birthday	78
Estate Sale?	80
Nineteen	81
Adoptee	82

Jazz Street   83

We Passed Books Around Too	85
Sam Brown	86
Jazz Improvisation	87
Finding Richie Havens	88
No TV	90
Breaking Up Over Indian Food With a Table Between Us	91
Yesterday's News	92
Singing the Blues	94
I Saw That Guy Today	95
B.B. King On Christmas Eve	96
Omega Poetry Workshop 2005	97
Running Into "Dr. K" At the Jazz Fest	98
Red Cross a Point Mint	99

Nonsense	100
Badi Assad Concert/High School Graduation	101
The Missing Poem	102
Bundle Of Jazz	103
Whit Smith	104
On the Way To Cedar Walton	105
Juanito Pascal	106
Little Jazz	107
AAA-Scrubs-Movie	108
Toasted Crumpet Croûtons	109
Press Conference With God	110
It's Not Just the Coffee	112
Becoming the Poem	114
You're Gone Again	115
About the Author	117

Dedicated to my husband, Lou, whose joy
makes my life more precious each day.
Thank you for listening to first drafts
aloud, for always finding the upside,
for a bottomless supply
of humor and smiles,
for believing in me.

*

Thanks to Susan Bright
for choosing to publish my work,
for your phenomenal expertise.

*

Thanks to my friend Ellie Jennings:
for calmly listening, proofreading.

*

Thanks to my father, who once
told me I should write a book,
and to my mother, who
encouraged me to
write this book.

*

Thank you to friends, family and teachers
who have been there for me as days of
our lives play out, on solid ground
and in my dreams. Thank you
for inspiring, encouraging,
listening, laughing,
and reminding
me to write
about that!

Introduction

You can make observations, journal all day and night; but a poem will emerge when it is ready. And it will rise up, like bread dough, after the proper amount of internal chemistry takes place. Like an old time pot of percolated coffee, which can't be poured until the bubbling up top ceases, it has to let go of the process. Even then, I often find, I have to let it calm down or chill a bit for a few days, weeks or months, so that when I look at it again, (again and again), it becomes more clear which words or lines are crashing the party and have to be escorted to the door.

A good poem is a revealing glimpse into our life, or the life of another, or into the subtle shifting of a season, or into the particular moment in a life that affected all the days and years that followed. It's a documomentary, to try a new word. Or as my young nephew, Evan said, "It's like a short story, but it's really really fast."

Getting to those moments can be gut-wrenching work. At the same time, it is a gift. To ignore that, or be lazy about the practice, is to dishonor the gift. Thanks to my mother, who introduced me to the library, and insisted I read in the summer, long before there were summer reading programs, and carried books everywhere we went, and gave books for presents when we were kids, I love reading great books as much as I enjoy writing.

To the wonderful writers I have met at Omega Institute, Taos Writing Salon and The Block Island Poetry Project off Rhode Island: Thank you for your passion, for honoring the practice and the work of writers who hear the call.

Where I'm From

I'll Never Dance With My Father

A few days before the wedding, Steve Piper,
our friend and photographer called to ask
a series of questions...such as who should
(or should not) be in a photo together; did
we want group shots or candid ones only;
did we want dressing room shots . . .

Simultaneously, my mother
was showing me her outfit,
confirming that her shoes
were okay with her dress.

One of Steve's questions took me by
surprise, made my throat close up:
Will you be dancing with your father?
My father had passed away
a year before I met Lou.
"No..." was all I could manage.

On my mother's way home in the car,
she was listening to a classical tape,
one that Dad had made, one
she'd never played through all the way.
There was a gap in the music, a few
words left there from a previous
recording...my Father's voice! She
called, breathless, at the discovery,
asked "Do you want me to play it over
the phone for you?" "Yes!" I said,
I think it's a message for me."

It was only these few words. He said,
*This, you'll have to do
on your own.*

Where I'm From

I come from a family of two parents and six siblings: one older brother, John, and two younger brothers, Pete and Bernie; and three younger sisters, Mary, Amy and Marti. We had one tortured cat, a rabbit who survived one summer and a parakeet who made it almost a year. We never had a dog. The Manions, a family with nine kids, lived in a house the back yard of which adjoined ours. They were our best friends.

We all went to St. Thomas the Apostle church on Sundays. Mom went every day. My dad tasted of coffee and buttered toast when I kissed him goodbye in the morning, his eyes lit up with hope and promise.

We lived close enough to Lake Ontario to feel the breeze and smell the rotting fish. Our simple house, in the center of a small circle street, grew with us as the years took us through the seasons. An empty lot across from our front yard was home to some tall Elm and Poplar trees. Between their branches, the sun set and the stars, ascending with our wishes, mesmerized our nights.

The neighborhood boys claimed the empty lot, built a substantial one-room wood fort for themselves. Once my mother sent me over to their bunker with a plate of sliced tomatoes, fresh from her garden. The boys were twelve or thirteen year olds hiding out with filched candy and cigarettes. All I remember is my embarrassment, their adolescent laughter.

The house had grown a family room, porch and a garage by the time Amy and Marti were blooming and I was reaching the end of high school. My parents said I could have a party senior year. It was the only mixed party I had in that house.

My parents appeared to stay out of the way – there was a French door between the family room and the rest of the house. We played all the popular music – the Beatles, the Beach Boys. Everyone was dancing and talking. We had soda, peanuts and cake. Later we got to the tried and true slow dances – *My Funny Valentine*, Johnny Mathis, The Lettermen.

Somehow word about the party got out to boys I didn't even know. Four or five guys from the "White City" neighborhood, near the lake, appeared with six packs of beer. Most of us were not drinking age yet; and even if we were, the "joint chiefs" would never have allowed it. So crashing with beer was way out of the question; what happened next was huge.

Dad, at six foot four, was the gentlest one in the family. His subtle sense of humor broke the ice with everyone—his kind, easy manner was his trademark. We were stunned when he appeared in the family room that night, picked up and pitched those party crashers, like they were bags of garbage, off the back porch.

All my girlfriends adored my father. Boys I went out and broke up with continued to ask how he was years later.

Years and years later, people still speak about this incident involving my father and the guys who crashed the party. No one remembers their names.

Email To Cleveland

Cleveland in the morning,
you in my heart.

Love you rockingly

L

*

Sent from my
BlackBerry
Wireless
Handheld

*

Dude,
The new
Capresso
begot
one shot
and died.

They're sending another.
Ground Hog Day
comes to mind.
   Oh, no, wait—
art imitates life!

Enjoy rock city.
miss you famously,

me

Another Business Trip

I hate the sound of your
suitcase zipper closing quickly
as time draws nearer
to your departure.

When you say goodbye
to Mystie, our cat, your voice
goes a slight notch higher.
The sound presses into
my chest. She doesn't
come to see you off,
like she does on
regular work days.

Soon you'll haul your baggage
down the stairs, which creak
their farewell as I inhale deeply,
waiting to hug you one last time,
to purse my lips as we make
funny faces, plan to talk
later—figure the time shift
between here and there.

You're too efficient at
  packing and leaving;
I'm able to sleep somehow.
We're too accustomed
  to separation. I envy
couples who never part.

Valentine

(for Lou)

Give me your
sense of adventure;
I'll share with you
  my heating pad.
Loan me your
Haruki Murakami;
I'll spot you in a
  shoulder stand.

I bake blueberry scones
for Sunday mornings;
  blend banana
  smoothies weekdays.
You add spice to
our weekly stir-fry,
do Saturday's errands
  at a nearby BJ's.

You unjam my little
brooding computer,
I nab your forgotten
  shirts from the dryer.
I sigh yawning at the
end of a very long day;
but you still have left
  one more smile.

Give me your sense of
  joy, my love, give me your peace.
In return you'll get half of my candy—
dark chocolate covered coffee beans.

This Time

This time I won't go into
   that dog scrap mode;
not gonna eat frozen vegetables
   till you come home.

It's weird when you leave me
   home all alone;
it's midnight in Japan when
   you call me at noon.

I'm going out for coffee
   every single day. Gonna
buy some brand new clothes;
   give the old ones away.

This time I'll go outside
   most every night—
I'll sing my backyard blues;
I'll nurse mosquito bites.

This time I'll pour myself
   a glass of wine, then
head straight out of town;
   won't even stop for signs.

This time I'll stretch out
   all my memories—
take them off the hook; hang
   them between two trees.

This time I'll ascertain
   the obvious: I'll
take my night mask off—
   I make no promises.

My Kin

My kin are gorgeous and thin
    on my Mother's side,
sweet, perky, petite Caseys
    all bones and smiles.

I always felt like a giant girl
    around them, so much
taller, hefty — an extrovert,
    leaving echoes behind.

When my Father's brother died,
    the other side of the family
gathered, near strangers — outside
    of the shared Heveron name.

But there they stood with my
    big thighs, sad Heveron eyes,
taller than floor lamps,
    refrigerators and coat racks.

One of my Father's nephews was
    nearly a twin to my brother,
Peter. They had my Dad's easy
    way of connecting with people.

They were our kin too; they wore our
    skin, and comfortable shoes.
They stood, with substantial thighs.
    And they all had our eyes.

Some of us buried our uncle Art that day;
    some said goodbye to their Dad.
Silently we grieved a long history —
    the one that we never had.

Leaves Leaving Summer

Today, at last, the summer
day we should have had –
pleasant enough to lie
in the hammock, read
a good book, watch
leaves leaving summer.
How divergently each one
takes its first and last dive.
One white bird passes through
a blue blanket of sky, as two
young squirrels race across
a telephone wire, just
saying hello.

One leaf spins
dozens of times
as it dances to death.
Another flutters by, left
then right, lowering itself
so gracefully that I'm stunned
when it slams into a garage roof
below, done sooner than expected,
  its elegant swan song.
Encouraged by the breeze,
an almond shaped leaf leaves
the tree, as if bored with its life,
drawing itself down, like a shade
at the end of the day. Another
one quits, as if it had just
checked its watch,
realized the time—
It was well after
five; took off for
leaf happy hour.

Birthday Dream in Rome

I woke up on my birthday,
remembering a dream in
which I was pulling a car out of
the driveway as Mom was pulling in
with guests I didn't expect. I went back
inside to tidy up. I was upstairs in my old
childhood room with the built-in dresser; and
Dad was there fixing things and cleaning up.

I knew Mom was down in the kitchen making
dinner. I said to Dad, "We don't realize all that
you're doing to help." He nodded. I said, "I don't
know what to do with all this stuff." Dad said,
    "That's okay - just do what you can."

The dream spoke to me on different levels.
Though Dad is gone, he is present, helping
behind the scenes. In spite of this wonderful
vacation, I prayed to die last night, after suffering
through a two-day torturous migraine headache that,
once it finally lifted, left me with a throat so swollen
I could not talk to Lou as we walked around Rome. It
finally occurred to me that I was allergic to something
in my travel bag. This had happened on another trip.
Once before, I was so overwhelmed with physical pain
that I prayed to die. But both times I awoke with
a vivid memory of a dream...a vision of my
Father gently encouraging me to press on
and enjoy all the beauty in life.

From out of this world,
the greatest birthday present.

Amnesty Email

Democracy
Democracy
Democracy
Demos
Kratos —
People
Rule.
Am I right?

This morning Amnesty
International phoned
to tell tales of horror
of US (United ? States)
picking suspects of terror
up from streets all over the
world, interrogating, jailing,
torturing without proof or trial.
They asked: Could we please help
again this new year with the hundred
dineros we gave last year? I said
"Nothing till tax return time."
And they said we have at
least four weeks after
getting a pledge card
in the mail. So I said
tho I can't promise;
I suspect you'll be
willing. So, in a
way, you are a
suspect. Don't
get caught.
love you with
freedoms,
I think.

Spaces

On Sunday morning,
her husband pours
maple syrup into
each concave
square of his
waffle, as if
he's finishing
a Monday New
York Times
Crossword
Puzzle.

On Friday nights, she
sighs at the chance
to finally *relax* with
him—holds a fine
glass of wine as
their favorite pasta
dishes are being
prepared. He tells
her for the hundredth
time about events in
his children's exceptional
lives, how they skipped
grades in school, left
early for college,
won every award.
He never stops smiling
recalling their past, she
waits for a.........gap,
a way to bring him
into the present,
the unknown future,
blank open spaces.

C & D Lawn No More

Cal died.
Jeff, the plumber told me.
No one knew he was sick,
not even his son Dave.
He just kept working till he
checked himself into a hospital
and died six weeks later.
He stopped
buying lawnmowers
two years earlier;
just sold the ones he had—
stopped taking care
of the building
who knows when—
a hundred holes in the roof
junk in the yard
he didn't seem to mind
raccoons and cats
birthing litters in the back,
squirrels playing circus
on his roof—
He always said hello
had his son mow my lawn,
plow the driveway—
I had to ask for a bill.
He was quiet in life
then he slipped
out of it silently
like the secret that he kept.

Maybe They Call it Spring

Maybe they call it Spring
because it's like a leap
      across a chasm
from Winter to Summer.

Maybe they call it Spring
since it's like a dream
      slipping away at the
shift from night to day.

You tighten your fluttering
      eyes against the light,
protesting the loss of your
      other life, no matter
how fractured or weird.
Night memories wiggle
out of the bed before you
find your feet on the floor.

Maybe they call it Spring
because it strings together
      opposite seasons, as
we sing out our dharma.

You fight off the darkness
at night...you check your
list, as your lids resist
the urge to rest. You don't
want to leave the day;
      it could be your last.
You plead one more icy
      glass of kitchen water.
Maybe they call it Spring
because the thrash of rain

is calling your name, back to
the Winter you want to forget.

You fight off the brilliance
      of noon day sun. You go
inside and hide in a book,
      (the original sun block).
One hour later you check
      the clock, change your
clothes, unwrap the hose,
take care of the garden.

Maybe they call it Spring
to draw your face to the earth,
where hyacinths break your
heart, like a one night stand.

Like circles upon circles,
maybe they call it Spring
repeating the lessons,
promising rebirth.

The Crying Room

Liz took the stairs to the
crying room, again and
again, her small child's
hand held no Kleenex,
purse, or indignation—
   only the attention
of her Mother's night out
at the *Cinema Theater*.
Down to the Ladies'
Room mirror, back up
to the noise proof booth,
filled with curbside couches
and chairs, a wooden crib,
a neighborhood ease
about snacks carried
in, crumbs left behind.

A different scene for sure,
than the old Sunday nights
she would walk there with
Bernie, a place to escape
the chores of home for
an hour or two and
dreams of a family that
might come to light...

So this is life with Lexie
at fifteen months...holding
her hand, taking the stairs to
the crying room, making faces
in the Ladies' Room Mirror.
Oh, yeah—what was the film?
Something about love, I think—
it was...something about joy.

I Wish You'd Met My Dad

Because you were subtle—
made a joke like my dad
I cried in Java's as I
reached for my hands.

"There's a gene," I read
"to cure hearing loss..."
"Which one," you asked
"Simmons?"
      (of KISS)
and I laughed . . .

then cried because
of my dad,
      my dad,
      my dad,
who would have
appreciated
      the joke.

"It was all I ever
needed," I said.

"It was all he ever
needed, too," said Lou.

The Airplane Shirt

I bought this turquoise print shirt
on June 6, 1986—the day before all
my peonies bloomed on Benton Street.
It was new, had a European label, *Longue
Distance*, cost me thirty dollars and I wore
it on my first date that night with George.
I don't remember where we went for dinner
or if we went out to hear music; I remember
we talked half the night. I remember cutting
an armload of peonies from the tiny front yard
for him to take to his mother on Sunday.
He showed up every single night
for about the next three years until
he finally asked me to marry him
and I said yes; and then said no.

I wore that shirt to the
Harmonic Convergence—
a day that was supposed to
bring a shift in consciousness
due to the sheer number of people
world-wide who were all meditating
on the shift simultaneously. I went to
the lake shore at dawn with a bunch of
other people to wait. Another day dawned.

Nothing visible happened;
but on that day, that was
supposed to be so special, my first
cousin, Doug Hagler, was on a flight
from Detroit, Michigan to Chicago, Illinois
for a job interview the next day. That plane
tragically crashed. He was killed in the crash,
along with everyone else who was on the airplane,
except for one lucky four year old girl whose life was spared.

When my parents told me,
what had happened, I
dropped my head in
sadness. Oddly
I noticed, for the
first time, that
the print on the
turquoise shirt was
a repeated pattern
of little black airplanes.

Broken Leg

Slip-on porch
    cry for help
wiggle toes
    bear weight?
pack of ice
    elevate
moan to sleep —

Next day
    X-Ray
whoa — fractured
    fib you la
purple cast
    pair of crutches
no instructions

stairs a bother
    skip a shower
take 3 Advil
    no, take more

Christmas cards
    stay indoors
answer phone
    lie on floor

read a book
    meditate
mantras, mudras
    healing, wait

friends and family
keep me straight.

After the Move

Three weeks after movers
loaded two whole households
into the mouth of a moving van,
and gang-planked it from the
      street straight through the
front door of our new Tudor home,
      an alarm clock surfaces—
from a box of washcloths,
      time stopped on its face,
like a cat, unexpectedly caught
      in its hiding place—
still as a cinder block.

In the bottom of a sewing
basket, I discover picture
      hangers and nails,
carefully removed and saved,
separately from the weight of
framed artwork they once
upheld. *The light is different
here*, a newly-merged collection
of art seems to say. We're
not sure where we want
to hang out yet.

Items we couldn't pack until
moving day dawn disappear
in the rush of departure, hide
out in unrelated genres of stuff,
amused by our attachments,
waiting for re-discovery, re-birth.

Inanimate objects, my eye!

Nearly Drowned

"Nearly drowned." Those are
the words I've always used
to describe a few moments
of my fifth year of life. Summer,
1953, my Mother, Lake Ontario
Beach, two brothers: one older, one
younger. Jean Lemperlee, our neighbor
from across the street. Me, bravely walking
out into the deepening water, up to my
bathing suit bottom, up to my waist,
up to my chest, no one calling me
back, it must be okay, up to my
shoulders, oh...up to my neck.
Whoa! Losing my footing!
Then spinning, I recall,
like a load of wash,
under the surface
of the lake I took
for granted.

It was decades later
when I asked my mother
why she wasn't the one who
saved me me that day. Why it
was Jean who pulled me out of
the water, who carried me back
to the blanket.

"That was you?" she whispered.

As if it happened that morning,
she recalled how some Bridge friends
happened to be having a luncheon
nearby, how she, awkwardly, ran

into them, her back to the lake,
a moment of inattention.

She said she must have been
holding my younger brother
in her arms. She grasped for
or guessed at the details.

I do not remember
if we had Abbotts
Frozen Custard
on the way home,
or if we told Dad
at dinner,
or, if we did,
what he said,
or how long it was
before we went back
to the beach again.

But her reply
left me
spinning,
like a lonely
load of laundry
in the lake
I'd always
trusted.

Onion Soup

I don't feel like crying/
but I am crying
onion/chopping
tears/
spilling/
from my/eyes
burning down my/
cheeks/
checking/
with my/
heart/
Is everything okay?

Please don't make
me cry/
onion chopping/
fears/
mincing /
all my/
pride/
dicing/
every pain/
changing/
my disguise./

Okay—I need a cry//
these onion tears/
are mine//
slicing through/the years//
mettle in different gears/
scraping all my truths—
straight into the kettle—
This gift I offer you—
this sweet and sour soup.

My Father's Car

I drive my father's Skylark;
        he doesn't need it anymore.
Dad flies invisibly nearby;
        I feel his presence in the car.

Once while rushing late to work,
I took the curve from
490 East to 590 North —
My left hand was resting on
        the steering wheel—
My right hand was dipping into
a box of Ritz crackers on the seat.

Abruptly my father's voice
        spoke clearly in my head.
To my daughterly astonishment,
        dig this - is what he said-

You don't know how thin the veil is
        between this life and the next—
You could be here in an instant!
Keep both hands on the steering wheel.

I drive my father's Skylark;
        he doesn't need it anymore.
He flies invisibly nearby;
I drive with both hands now.

I feel Dad's presence
        in my heart:
He loves me
        and that car.

KJ2P 88

As I exited the Webster post office,
a smiling gentleman stopped by
my car and asked: "So who is KJ2P?"

"Oh, are you a HAM?" I asked.
He gestured to his Ham radio license
plate, rattled off his call letters...
"My dad," I said— "I couldn't keep
the HAM plate after he died . . ."
"So you ordered a vanity plate
with his call letters," he smiled.
"Exactly," I nodded, "and added 88,"
"For *love and kisses*," he said, kindly.
"I knew him—Hev—Heveron?
        ...Jack Heveron."
"Yes! Jack Heveron!" I said excited.
"Up in Irondequoit!" he said. "Ferl-?"
"Farrell Terrace!" I said, thrilled.

"He was a charming man, your father."
"Yeah, he was," I said—"Still Is...
    I'm glad I kept the plate;
      you're the first one who's asked."
"No kidding," he said, pleased for the moment.

"What's your name?" I asked then.
"Abe—Abe Goodman," he said
    A Good Man, I thought.

When I returned to the car,
  the windshield was hazy.
"Is that you all fogged up?"
  I whispered.
Searching for the defrost knob,
    I headed off to work.

A Buddhist Waits For Easter

In the Zen Center Women's Changing
Room, after the early morning sitting,
I remarked to a young woman I'd not
seen before how cold it was that day.
She wrote in a tiny notebook, held
up to me, "I don't believe we've met."

I extended my hand, "I'm Elaine."
        She wrote, "Heveron?"
To my astonished look, she wrote,
        "I know Brian." Hand
to heart, I smiled, "my nephew."
        She wrote, "I'm Deidre."

I asked her if she was deaf.
She shook her head, flipped to
page one of her miniature diary
        which read, "Until Easter,
I won't be speaking...I will try
and be as clear as possible."

"You're giving up speaking...for Lent?"
        She nodded with a broad smile.
"That's a huge sacrifice," I noted,
        stating the obvious.

She wrote something about the impact
        of sound on her in this absence.
"So—you're a musician?" I asked
She held her hands up to the left
        of her face, played
        an imaginary flute.

The Pair

In 1969, a young couple is married by a
Justice of the Peace in *Monterey, California*.

The groom's father happens to be
        in Caracas on a business trip.
His Venezuelan host orders from Boston
        a small gift for the newlyweds:
a salt shaker and pepper mill set
in white enamel, with a black screen-
        printed Chicago street scene.

Sadly, by the time the gift arrives,
        two and a half months later,
        the couple has separated
        for reasons beyond words.
The bride is told by the mother of the groom:
"Just keep the gift; they wouldn't understand."

Twenty-five years later, as the woman is
placing the salt shaker into a box
        of items to be donated to a
women's shelter, she receives word
that her former husband has died.

The upside down pepper mill,
        still in her hand,
reveals for the first time,
etched in metal on the
        bottom of the set:
Made in *Monterey, California*.

She removes the salt shaker from the box.
Sitting alone, she grinds black pepper
        onto her summer salad.

Omega Massage

How could I not accept
the gift of silence
the therapist was
offering to me—

I wanted to converse—
to connect with words
to find her soft spot,
her brand of humor.

She stood her little ground
in her beige jumper dress
          as I laid face-down
in my nakedness.

Slowly, her strong hands
          untied the knots
which had built up
inside of me—

All I could do was breathe
          and release my
          judgment of her,
let her strange love in,
          like lavender lotion,

permeating the air,
          like a yawn that
stretches out a moment
          too full of caring.

Coyote Man

She finds his silence
mystifying, frustrating and
liberating — all at once;
he asks for nothing.

He envelopes her in warmth
and makes quick departures.

He stays in touch with her heart,
but never speaks of the future.
He only knows
what he's always known.

Independence, solitude, singularity,
his coyote-man cave-room bed.

Yet instinctively he finds her
tenderest spots — the untouched places;
and dares to quietly unwrap
the buried treasures of her heart.

And then, in darkness,
he gently, silently
places his hands
on her very soul.

How It Is To Be Retired

Like my friend Shae said,
*We can't give you any
    more time than this.*
What will six Saturdays
and a Sunday feel like—
What does a non-working
woman do with her day?

This is how it is
to be retired—to be free
from Xerox, excused from
reporting to a manager of my time.

As I transition from *stuck here*
to: *all the things I ever wanted to do*,
I begin to tread an unknown path:
What will become of this indefinite hitch?

An imagined epoch turns out to be
a series of distractions bidding for
my attention, waiting for the wave
that could take me out to sea.

My permanent break:
When I have some time
begins now. My final
    age is unknown,
but it's coming up.

I've got my number from the
bakery counter dispenser:
"Fifty-eight? Fifty-eight?
    Is there a fifty-nine?"

You Can't File a River Away

You don't always have
to be a rock. It's okay
    to spill your feelings.
You asked, "Where do I
put this?" I guess the only
    answer is nowhere man.
    You can't file a river away
like some invoice or envelope,
    El, you must simply let it flow.

I wish he had the guts to follow
his heart. How can he call to say
"I miss you so — think of you always."
and not realize it's going to to topple
that fragile wall you've built up again?
That is some karmic debt, my friend.

He has the map to
your heart and soul;
you've got a shared secret
history, the things only you two
know about each other. What do you
do with that? To whom will you leave
that when you're gone? How do you
manage to hold it all in your huge
generous heart and home with-
out a lease, without a destiny?

As your heart breaks again
and again, I send healing
thoughts your way; and I
pray for the dimming of
a bright, but damaging
light in your life.

Peter

Your feet firmly planted
on the ground,
your legs a pair of oak trees,
your chest lifted broadly
in some hip shirt —
your eyes reveal the smile
your beard can hide.

You ingest knowledge
and exude talent,
depth of heart,
respect for all things.
You work inside yourself;
you ask humbly.
You are so patient.

Dreams manifest through your hands
You can coax gemstones or rocks,
leather, cement or tiles—a piece of land
to start a new life — transform into
something amazing, magical,
functional, unique — a solar castle
and water falling deep in the desert.

No wonder the lakes freeze,
glass smooth, soliciting you
with your skates
to come for a spin.
No wonder the mountain,
dressed up in snow,
calls you by name,
welcomes you home.

Bernie

You had just turned seven years old
when I was fifteen and my first date,
Tony Mangione, arrived at our house.
I was nervous then mortified as
you appeared in the family
room grinning, "Hey Tony—
Say something in Italian!"
He just laughed, gave you
a quick chin up nod,
said: "Hey brush cut!"

Years later I came home
from Florida for a week.
You invited me to
come over and hang
out with your musician
friends. We all smoked
back then and it seemed
like we smoked one thin
cigarette after another
while you guys decided
what tune to practice next.

I've seen and heard you play
hundreds of times since then
in dozens of venues. Always,
you give me a special look or
nod when I arrive. And you
respect your instruments like
they are your brothers, sisters,
children — they bring out your
light — and the music you make
    together is so darn sweet.
It is always so so sweet.

Going Deaf

I still dream that I work in the
   Happy Note record store,
spinning vinyl all day, filing
albums from A to Z in jazz, rock
and blues, ordering new albums,
helping customers, all the while
listening, listening, listening
   'til my ears start ringing
from non-stop music.

We discovered new artists and
   wore out our favorites. We
   memorized lyrics, read all
the liner notes. We even carried
   rare brands of guitar strings
our adored artists preferred.

We sold music, talked music,
   and in our free time —
we went to concerts.
We saw the Crusaders and
were deafened by the Cars.
We went to see films like
The Last Waltz, singing
along with The Band.

I wake up today, twenty-
   four years later and I
can't hear the phone ring,
   can't hear the water
   running in the sink.
I cannot hear the tea
   kettle whistling
on the kitchen stove.

A Moment Remembered At Corpus Christi

My black glove
in a black man's hand
was all I saw at first,
then the crutches,
then the one leg.

This gentle,
sad-faced man
with only one leg
      had stopped
to pick up my glove
from the aisle floor
      in church
to return it to me.

Dear Dad

I ache
to see you again.
I long for even a
foggy
dreamscape.

As spring transforms
the landscape,
my heart is pierced
again
and again
with autumn's
ruthless recall
of you:
and no one is here
to nurture me through
but Jesus.

Autumn Without You

for Dad

Ghostly corn plants
wave
their brown translucent
remnants
in brisk November
breezes.

Tall gracious sunflowers
bow their heavy heads
respectfully
in silence.

Masses of colorful leaves,
now underfoot and crisp—
leave delicate
heightened branches
to etch their recent
memories
in the backdrop
of the sky.

You Go Girl

Carol's Tights

You gave me some tights you no longer wear,
        to cut in half, to pull up over my cast
        my fiberglass leg.
"They're fun," you said, as you offered me
        the bag of sundry stockings
        in two shades of purple,
        textured off-white,
        Raggedy-Ann striped.

At home, I gathered the mesh of them to
my face, smiled when I drew in your
scent. Softly they revealed cigarettes,
perfume, cedar, and strength.
        I inhaled and held in your house, your
        songs, an array of straw stars in your
entrance way, stained glass window, your
        worn kitchen floor, your
        children's photos, your
        bright red bench, your
        aestival gardens, your
        exiting doors.

How would I cut them apart when they held your
        dint, your drive, your cogency, your
walk downtown, the way you frame your
        days and nights, your
        recent decisions, your
grandchildren's Christmas, your
        great loving friends,
        your yesterdays.

Snapshot For a Birth Mother

> *Washington, D.C.*
> *April 17, 1952*
> *It's a Boy*

For whatever reason
Miss, you endured the nine
months and pain of labor
I thank you for your time.

Were you even eighteen
when you traded him to
Jewish Family Service
for empty-armed freedom?

Your Portuguese weekend-
  lover did not ever
know he sired a son you
cut loose to strangers.

Do you want to see the
  boy as he came to be—
a man of joy, his eyes
gleam like a baby's eyes.

He kissed me ten times this
  fantastic spring morning
and he laughed at my—"How
can you leave for work now?"

There's not a day I don't
think about you, Miss, with
bliss in my heart, I thank
  you for carrying him...
  I thank you for sparing
your son, who loves me more

than any other man
I have known before.

There's more to this picture:
  he gave life to two boys
who have endured their own
losses with strength and with poise.

Resemblances carried,
(see what you have started).
They are happily married
to women who love them.

Close your brimming eyes Miss:
  I hope you can hear this:
   Your gift was so generous!
Words can't thank you enough.

Transformations

for Pat P.

We were the same sex then.
You suffered through monthly
cramps, like all the women
we knew. You had a code
of ethics, a *girlfriend*,
one sister, five brothers,
parents, grandparents, friends,
dreams, an odd combination
of comfort and dis-ease with
who you were physically.

You never judged anyone
and, the way I remember it,
no one judged you when you
decided to change genders.

We carried giant film
boxes over our heads,
drew impositions, bribed
schedulers with chocolate,
protected little transparencies,
tissue-covered reflective art.

We hand-delivered freshly
typeset lines of hype, rushed
  revised mechanicals,
like they were living organs,
to the art department, shuttling
camera proofs to the salesmen,
overnighted them to customers
who "Fed-Xed" them back again.

Final proofs were transported
in a huge white envelope,
curiously referred to as
The Gray Envelope. Then,
in a dark room called Stripping,
thirty men sat whistling
different tunes, a cacophony
like the Rochester Philharmonic
Orchestra before a concert begins.

We waited for more approvals,
Blueprints, Match prints,
Chromalins. We created
over-sized paste-ups, OK's-
to-Print, while dinosaur-
sized presses ran twenty-
four hours a day, seven
days a week. We were
hard pressed to keep up.

In the morning we burst through
the Bindery area doors, checking
cutting, stitching, punching.
We chased finished jobs out
the shipping dock doors to
hysterical customers.

Every day was the *end
of the world*, if promised
dates were broken. Rarely
did we meet those dates.
(Why we kept promising
the impossible is a
printing mystery.) Any
given hour eighteen things
could (and did) go wrong;

but ninety-five percent
of them could be fixed one
way or another for the
cost of more precious time.

After the annual reports,
once a year, we were
treated to the *Rio Bamba*
or *Edwards* for dinner.
Sometimes a caring sales
person posted a Thank You
letter, some customer
took the time to write,
(our absolutely
favorite reward).

We were the same sex then.
You honored me when you
let me keep your secret
for a year while you
were evaluated by
a known psychologist.
After that, the hormone
shots began and eventually
three surgeries. While one
of our friends was sadly
losing a breast to the curse
of cancer, you couldn't
wait to get rid of your
healthy breasts.

Your voice lowered as your
eyes lifted to steady contact
with others as you found
your way easily into a man's
world. Why I never took

photos of you as a woman
escapes me now as I notice
your receding hairline.
Somewhere I have a snap-
shot of you at a company
picnic. You used to wear
miniature earrings, with
your short hair, khaki pants
and button-down shirts.

Everyone knew at some point
in time. You were shaving.
We were starting to use *he*
instead of she. I remember
asking why you didn't grow
a mustache to make it easier
on us. You said because it would
be too hard on your grandmother.
Your life's huge dream attained;
but kindness and respect for
your elders' wishes prevailed.

Those years were full of farewells
as our merged companies'
employment dwindled from
fifteen hundred to 500 people.
Week after week, we filled
The Portico after work
having snacks and wine,
saying goodbye to someone.

Those years were full of celebrations
as well. We had surprise
lunchtime Wedding and Baby
Showers, we took up collections,

chipped in on gifts, played
practical jokes on each other.

The most unforgettable day was
the one when several giggling women
grabbed and pulled on your left arm,
and begged you to come with us,
one last time, to a Baby Shower
at *The Portico Restaurant*.

But before you could say no,
        some of the men
took your right arm and said,
        "He's one of us now;
and we go to *Roncones*
        for lunch on Fridays."

You went comfortably on with
the men, as we witnessed
a departure that day,
like no other
departure
before.

Garage Sale Item #1

In April of 1983,
   a young, playful
Jewish woman
   buys a dazzling
rhinestone
   Christmas tree pin
at a garage sale
in Johnson City,
Tennessee.

She mails it,
   as a birthday gift
to her *Shiksa* girl-
   friend, who lives in
Coconut Grove, Florida.

The two friends
eventually lose
track of each other.

Twenty years later,
somewhere in
   upstate New York,
the friend takes the pin
   out of her jewelry box,
as she does
   every December,
pins it to a red
   velvet jacket,
and wears it to a
   Christmas party.

Flying Home from Rome

On the flight home from Rome,
a teenager across the aisle from
me is entertaining herself for
half an hour looking at, and
playing with, ice in a glass.
In between this activity, she
spends time looking at her
own hands, as if these are
new and fascinating experiences.
I am entertaining myself watching
her. She's wearing Doc Martins, black
jeans and a navy hoodie. Discreetly,
I watch her dig a hole into the top of
a dinner roll. She then pushes the
top of a small carrot into the
bun. It looks like a breast.
She seems quite alone in
her fantasy world. I wait
until I have to get up,
then say, "Excuse me,
but is that a Janet Jackson
bun?" She completely breaks
   up laughing, crimson-faced,
turns the bun over and says,
   "You've ruined my meal."
I realize, at that moment,
how much I absolutely
love making someone
laugh. And there is
something really
fantastic about
making a
stranger
laugh.

Blank Canvas

for Sheila Lytle

Why won't you paint? Why can't you see —
the noise you hear is the hungry cry
of blank canvas. Why do you hold
your vision hostage from this easel?

You prepare and study, build,
re-arrange, polish and stack.
Your place is holy with serenity as
daylight wanes, another winter looms.

Won't you mother this foster child canvas?
Take it in your arms; give it a lovely name?

Won't you layer the sky in sunrise?—
recalling how it looked
the morning after
you first made love?

Before the last fuchsia blossom gives
up the idea of flight, won't you kiss its
bleeding colors from your healing lips,
lay it out in timelessness,
brush it off your list?

And when you burn your tenderness
into this easeled canvas
will you varnish it in trust?
Frame it in release?

Then will you swing open
your studio door,
setting it free to
find a new home?

Garage Sale Item #2

Five minutes before guests
    are to arrive for dinner,
an older man surprises his
younger wife with an exquisite
necklace of cut turquoise stones.
The dinner is successful;
    but the marriage ends
eight months later.

Twelve years later,
    in another state,
the divorced woman
places the turquoise necklace
    on the corner of a table
at a garage sale.

A woman passing by
stops,
    lifts up the necklace,
surprised at its weight,
    asks "How much?"

The seller shrugs,
"It needs a new life –
    25 cents."

The woman passing by
quickly gives the divorcee
    2 dimes and a nickel,
puts the necklace on,
    and wears it
for the rest of her life.

Not Her Boyfriend

for Rita and Don

He's not her boyfriend, he is much more
than that. Not just her lover or her lad.
More than a sweetheart—he's her man.

He's no Casanova, and not a Don Juan.
Lothario doesn't work. More than a flame
or a gallant; he's her gentleman.

Not her crush, her steady, or her weekend
fellow. Not an esquire, a seducer, or a
gigolo! They're in this thing together—
The word is he's her beau!

More than her suitor, or her wooer—
(courter is out of date); paramour sounds
too uppity, partner sounds a little gay.

Mate is too British; Caballero too Spanish;
Sheik is too mysterious; Romeo is simply tragic.

Old man is too demeaning. Cavalier—too cavalier!
He's more than a *swain*; He's her *beloved* I hear.

We searched every resource, to find a *boyfriend* synonym.
Only the Italians have the perfect term.

He's her *Inamorato*—
He's the one she loves.

It's perfectly romantic—
this hard-to-find word
for the one who came along
and re-arranged her world.

Dance Recital – Tap I

The little white umbrella slipped
from your hand down to the floor;
but you kept right on dancing,
like a professional grown-up star.

You saved your tears for later;
      you held your head up high—
bolstering an invisible umbrella
      up to the imaginary sky.

This was not what you wanted to happen;
      but you did the best you could:
you let those proverbial raindrops
      just keep falling on your head.

You stayed focused on the dance group
      in your yellow slicker coats.
You bravely finished the dance.
      Our hearts were in our throats.

I don't even know what your name is;
      but you are a heroine to me—
'cause you continued to tap dance,
      when you must've wanted to flee.

Girl, I'll think of you in my future,
      when I start to slip or fall
I'll remember your illusive umbrella
      and how it protected us all.

Earrings

On *Alitalia*, all the stewards and stewardesses are wearing striking black leather gloves. Lou is sleeping as I muse about the business of accessories. He wonders why I spend precious time choosing which earrings, necklaces, scarves, or hats to pack for a trip. He is always ready to go ahead of me.

I tell him that I need, *women need*, to feel a certain comfort when we leave home. It's not just about matching colors or being warm enough, and it does not matter if we are *only* going to be around strangers. Indeed, accessories have their own energy, which, like perfume, will attract simpatico souls.

On this trip, I bought silver and turquoise earrings Amy found in Mexico for me years ago, Japanese mother-of-pearl ones from Jody, a long pink scarf Susan picked up in Nepal, a purple felted hat which Mary McStravick made. I had fun placing that hat on the head of any statue I could reach and taking snapshots. When we returned, I placed the photos on her office door at work.

We were thousands of miles from home at a street festival in Salsomaggiore, Italy, on Easter Sunday, when I said to Lou, "I can't believe we haven't run into anyone we know — there are so many people here!" He laughed, shook his head at such a crazy presumption.

A half hour later, a woman's voice called out from the crowd: "Elaine!!!!" It was Marie Ninkov, my favorite yoga student, who had given me earrings as a gift when I stopped teaching. I was wearing those very earrings when she called out my name.

Betsy

> for Betsy O' Flynn

I never come to your venison roasts;
   you never buy my books.
We send each other Christmas cards,
   news and snapshots of the kids.

The years go by since those long days
   we worked in propinquity –
producing brochures and catalogs
   in the printing industry.

You were the company observation deck
   with your ears to the wall at all times.
I never understood it all
   'til I heard of your early life.

Your father's business travel was a lousy lie –
   he had another *family* in a town nearby!
When he disappeared on Christmas Day,
   your Mom must've closed her eyes.

I hadn't seen you in many years
   when my own father died, but
you found your way to the funeral parlor.
   You stood there by my side.

I never come to your venison roasts;
   the years go by and by. But you
were there when it mattered the most.
   You're still a friend of mine.

I've Got Your Eyes Today

Mary always rubs her eyes....
Dad once said it was because her eyes
were so big, everything kept falling in.

I've got your eyes today:
—things keep falling in!
Leaning over the sink,
   I let loose lashes,
strings, hunks of dirt,
gossip, crumbs I left
   for the squirrels
that they turned away,
commentary on the
   news of the day,
pop-up windows, litter
that needs to be changed,
recipes I don't have half
   the ingredients for,
snow tires I meant to
   drive to the dealer,
a charity spreadsheet
due to my C.P.A. brother,
my ripped rough drafts,
banana peels en route
to a frozen compost heap
outside, tapes I plan to
convert to CDs, un-
stamped birthday
cards of the week,
cloudiness creeping
into late afternoon
before I've had time
to seriously consider
my plans for the day.

Black Currant Tea

She hadn't been
      with a man
in at least two
years, when she
asked him to come
up that Christmas.
Only he could make
that day perfect.
In her mind, she sang
a rhythm and blues song
by Ace Spectrum called
*Don't Send Nobody Else
(If You Can't Come Yourself)*.

They'd been endless lovers
in Miami, in New York, in
  the past. Touch and scent
preceded sight. She never even
saw him coming at the airport gate
in his brimmed black urban cowboy
hat—shading his eyes, black leather
pants. He threw his arm around
her and they just kept walking
towards Baggage Claim, like a four-
legged creature with a shared mission.

Outside of her bedroom
door, he handed her a
furry little Ram on wooden
legs, a gorgeously printed
Book of Sushi by Tachibana,
and a precious gold tin
of black currant tea,
whose intoxicating scent
would give her comfort for

months after he left.
She gave him a finely-
honed oak Kaleidescope
with dazzlingly bright
polished glass stones.

A week after he left, he called to tell her:
"That was the best Christmas of my entire life,"
then added: "including my childhood."

It was ten years before she saw him again
for the last time. Inconceivably,
they were not meant, and did
not need, to be together.

It was seven more years after that,
before she bought a tin of
black currant tea again.
She heated up water in
the tea kettle, poured it
over the leaves and inhaled
the exotic scent as
she sipped the nectar.

That same day, he picked
up the oak Kaleidescope
from a bookshelf in his office,
looked true North through
the dazzlingly bright
polished glass stones.

And she could see the colors;
And he could smell the tea.

Native American Dental Assistant

She always talks about cruises
  when I see her, twice a year.
She's fair-skinned with bleached
blond hair. She cleans my teeth.

As her hands invade my mouth, she speaks
about Caribbean shores she visits with her sisters.
This time, she tells me, she might have to go to
Canada, with her husband and kids,
to the *Mohawk Reservation*, where her father
grew up. I nearly fall off the dental chaise
lounge. She adds: "He's only a small
percentage Native American."

Envious, I raise my eyebrows, mumble
"Still!!" Half talking to herself, she says
"I never re-registered on the reservation
in my married name or registered the kids. . .
They're at that age now. . .they're getting curious
about their background. I don't know. . .
everything is so commercial. At the Reservation
store, if you buy something and turn it over,
it probably says *Made in Taiwan*."
Then she says: My father doesn't even *look* Indian."
"Still!" I insist, as she raises the chaise up
for me to rinse. "It's in your blood, go there!
Get some Native American literature;
teach your children."

I don't say it,
but I wonder,
if in six months,
when I return,
those black roots
will be all grown out.

Sister

Were you ever a cheerleader, Mary?
I can't remember now.
You have that pep team spirit —
that optimistic style.

You brought us to Mingo Lodge,
began an annual fall affair —
Covewood at Big Moose Lake —
Ah! the Adirondack mountain air.

You sprung Saratoga Springs —
  (they have jazz festivals there!)
Took us to dinner at Chez John Pierre —
brought Spanish and French students here.

You carry envelopes, projects,
formidable plans — your calendar
        is substantially jammed.
Still there are pockets of time
for every project you choose.
You love all the people, their stories,
the barter, the chaos, the news.

Your heart breaks in empathy
        when someone you know,
even casually, endures a
        painful loss.
You inhale, remembering
your own losses in silence;
but count your blessings
out loud, with a sigh
and a cheerleader's smile.

Muriel's Place

Muriel's place was my citadel in the seventies. Before I knew her very long, I felt totally at home with her. After work, on the way home, I would stop by her place, even if I had a headache. Her relaxed warmth and welcoming presence always made me feel better, no matter who else was around.

She had lived in England from age 15 to 25 and never lost her British accent. Once she invited me to go over with her; but I couldn't afford the air fare. She brought me a studded blue velvet pant suit that was unlike anything I've ever seen. I wore it for years.

Times when I was feeling emotionally lousy, Muriel would turn me on to a new philosophy book that would lift me out of a funk, get me smiling and enthused about life again. She always had a fresh perspective. She had an amazing peacefulness about her, like a rock in a stream. My touchstone.

Muriel was the last person I saw when I left Miami in 1980. It was twenty-seven years before I saw her again. On a recent short trip to South Florida, I called to see if she was free for coffee or lunch. She had just had surgery on her jaw; but in a garbled way, she managed to say, "You're not coming twelve hundred miles and not seeing me — you have to come by! I want to meet Lou too." Though the years and the recent surgery had been hard on her, she was still my warm and positive friend. She had survived cancer and had a portion of her jawbone removed, replaced with bone from her own pelvis and tissue from her breast. She wore a pink bathrobe and looked like she'd just had her hair done. Her eyes were bright, welcoming and ready to laugh through obvious encumbrances.

We'd kept in touch through letters, birthday and Christmas cards, the occasional phone call. I knew her stepfather had died. Her father from birth had died when she was young. She said to her mother, "It's so sad...now I have no father; both of them have passed."

For some reason her mother lost control and revealed a long-kept secret. "You don't know who your father was," she snapped, "Your father was a rapist." It was like a slap: hard, fast, unthinkable.

Muriel's mother married the man Muriel knew as her father; they looked like most families with love, support. Why her mother had kept this secret was understandable.

Why her mother blew her cover just before she died is baffling. Why did Muriel's expression of loss invoke this ugly revelation? Did her mother resent the feeling of loss Muriel had for her fathers?

Now Muriel wakes up mornings a bit nauseous, recalling events in her life, trying to re-align them with this new reality.

Seal and Barry

"You're going to always
be honest and fair,
when you're naked in a tub
of hot water with your lover."

In the seventies, in Miami,
before I owned a car, my
friend Seal Nunemaker
gave me rides to work. Each
day her husband, Barry, gave
her three one dollar bills:
one for breakfast, one
for lunch, one for gas.

Seal was petite with braided
long red hair, brown eyes,
and outstanding freckles.
Her elfish smile was neither
flirtatious nor innocent when
she breezily asked the gas
station attendant each day for
"One dollar's worth please."

We often stopped at a restaurant
where we'd order two eggs,
buttered toast, grits and
bacon for ninety-nine cents.
Seal always squeezed the
juice from a slice of lemon,
    onto her grits for flavor
and grinned at the brilliance
of all that extra taste for free.

Seal popped into my mind
recently, as I rummaged

through the refrigerator
for a fresh lemon to slice.
I tried to recall if we even
had the money back then
to tip the waitress;
I can't remember.

What I do remember was
asking Seal once what made
her so happy, what made her
marriage work with Barry.

Eyes sparkling, impish smile
widening her face, she said:

"Well, we have this deal . . .
if we have a problem
to work out between
us, we run a hot bath,
. . . take off
all our clothes,
and discuss it
in the bathtub.
You're going to always
be honest and fair, when
you are naked in a tub of
hot water with your lover."

As I slice into my lemon,
I know in my gut that
Seal and Barry are still
together. They had
a good deal.

Sixtieth Birthday

for Chris Barry

May you have sixty perfect days
a romantic evening sky—
      sixty billion stars
      sixty restful sighs.

Into sixty yoga poses you'll fold,
with varying sequences each day
good strength in all your bones,
peace and calm regarding . . . *age*.

We've seen sixty ways you roll your eyes
with your fantastic dimpled grins,
as you try on six different outfits, whispering:
"Does this make me look thin?"

May there be sixty dollars in your wallet
      for every time you have sighed
to be used on massages and pedicures
      until all your old tears have dried.

May you find a sixty percent markdown
      on every antique you find
      and win a game of Ping Pong
with a wonderful sixty-hit stride.

You'll show us sixty sexy dance moves—
a salsa star on a smooth dance floor
while sixty friends raise their glasses
clapping and singing "One more!"

You'll relish sixty sumptuous new
appetizers, while B.B. sings the blues...
as you recall your favorite punch lines
while you friends laugh and schmooze.

May you find sixty blossoms in your garden
for every loss you have ever known
a subtle, yet beautiful reminder
of all the love you've sewn.

I wish you sixty reasons to accept
the person who you are today—
sixty memories to cherish always
and sixty you can toss away.

As you listen to the music today
and hear all your favorite songs,
may you remember all the lyrics
so you can easily sing along.

I wish you sixty hugs and kisses
        and thrilling things to do—
the return of sixty thousand smiles
        we've all received from you.

Estate Sale?

A sign out front read:
Everything Must Go!
Every item in the modern
Brighton home was for sale.

Shae's brown eyes and
designer's heart coveted
a stylish multiple-drawer
Chinese chest. The lawyer
part of her drove a hard bargain
as she examined the smooth
pull of its novel drawers,
scrutinized its dove-tailing:
this show piece had better
stand up to its keen looks.

Leaving the sellers hanging,
Shae drove off, considering
whether to buy or not to buy.
I pulled up next to her car
at the red light ahead.
"They shouldn't have billed
it as an Estate Sale," she called
from her window. "It is false
advertising for an ordinary
neighborhood household sale."

Perhaps it was premonitional,
I thought, since, at *some* point,
       Everything Must Go.

Now, an elegant Chinese chest,
from an ordinary household sale,
warmly welcomes Shae's guests
as they arrive at the estate.

Nineteen

The term hadn't even been coined yet
when she was *date-raped* at nineteen.
You told her you were 25 years old
and divorced; but you were 31,
had a wife and two kids.

It was supposed to be a pleasant ride
around the lake in your cabin cruiser,
laughing and waving to other boat-owners;
but she lost her virginity and sanity at once
in a hostile heart-pounding acquisition.
You threatened her—
"It's a long swim home, college girl."

There was no Rape Hot Line back then—
and therapy was uncommon.
Shame overwhelmed her; surely
God had condemned her—
she turned away from Him
for a very long time.

Thirty-three years later,
        she asks herself this:
Did you ever have a nightmare
of her fists pounding
        your chest,
her blood and her tears?

And did you remember
        her scream
when your daughter
        turned nineteen?

Adoptee (after John Engman)

There is a child who makes
the stars come out at night.
That's how a poem should start.
Don't say: we waited two years to adopt her
        and then had only three days to drive
        to the next town to bring her home,
like a dish to pass, just in time for Easter.

Don't say you never thought about racism
coming your way when you checked
a small box on a form. Interracial __yes.
Say the love you imagined was only
        a drop of rain in the ocean.
Say she is the light of day.
Say she is the speed of light.
Say she is the ground
        on which angels play.
You teach her music;
        she shows you the dance.

Don't say you miss walking alone
        with your husband every night,
tidying up the house, before slipping
into the bedroom to make love,
door wide open—then sleeping
        a blessed eight hours.

Say she keeps us young and laughing
Say she teaches patience and understanding.
Say only this child could show you
what things in life are key.
Don't say: We miss our friends.
Say: she is our guru, our dharma.
        our greatest blessing.
She makes the stars come out.

Jazz Street

We Passed Books Around Too

It wasn't just sex, drugs and
  rock and roll, you know...
  throughout the seventies.
We passed books around too:

Ram Dass, Krishnamurti, Alan Watts,
  Fritz Perls, Eric Fromm, Kahlil Gibran
Gurdjieff, Ouspensky, Rogers,
  Yogananda, Lobsang Rampa,
Edgar Casey, Carl Jung.

In rooms divided by strings of beads,
we placed red light bulbs in our lamps,
   sat cross-legged on the floor,
burning hand-made candles and
Nag Champa incense. We tried ethnic
food, sprouts, and astral projection.

As we inhaled and held in the smoke,
we read every album cover liner note,
as we listened, *just listened* to music.
We studied our chakaras and dreams,
Transcendental Meditation, hatha
Yoga, the Bhagavad Gita.

There was a shift, the
      lift of a curtain,
There was an opening —
        We took the passage.

Sam Brown

> *Concert for George Harrison, November 29, 2002*
> *Royal Albert Hall in London*

I want to be Sam Brown—
for just two minutes; yes—
I want to sing that song;
I want to wear that dress!

She rises from the stage—
of stars, the mother lode.
She turns back time, sweet Lord;
she's young and hot, she's bold!

She leaps up with the words—
the lines her trampoline.
Dhani is by her side—
the Royal Albert scene.

She throws her purple hat
mid *Horse to Water* song—
space hangs between the words—
back-up gals keen along.

She must've paid her dues—
could sing her father's blues.
She has the hippest moves—
where did she get those shoes!

She flashes perfect teeth;
she has the greatest eyes.
For just two minutes please—
give me Sam Brown's disguise.

Jazz Improvisation

for Steve Greene

You're a star-feather rhinoceros—
you tie your shoes with dental floss.
You carry alphabet soup in your pocket
to remember your name.

You are an ethereal conglomerate
of mucous, pain, hardware,
high hilarity, and burning chaos.
Only nonsense enlightens you —
only nonsense arranges you.

You take no prisoners, but you
brake for sad faces and weird energy.
Your car seats are covered with amplifiers,
kale, and rice with mayo, extra socks.

A student takes notes as you gently escort an insect
out of the studio — down 200 flights of stairs.
Later you promise a raccoon your best china,
if he will come visit your trailer at 3:00 a.m.
(He comes for the foot massage.)

You have 47 best friends
and half a million students worldwide.
You realize every phone call; it's never the right time.
You wake up at eleven and pirate the nighttime.

You write songs on tree bark;
   and you make your mark.
You leave four thousand notes one morning.
   They all say "Thank you."
"Thank you." "Thank you very much."

Finding Richie Havens

One splendid night in 1968, Richie
Havens sang two songs on
Johnny Carson's Tonight Show:
Something Else Again
and *Don't Listen To Me*.
Hearing his rich voice and the
love messages he had to convey
somehow woke up my spirit.

Mickie and I were college sophomores
       but we didn't even own a stereo.
The next day after classes, I took two
buses and walked to a downtown Sears
store. To my amazement, in their puny
record department, they had Richie's
album, *Something Else Again*.
I handed it to the clerk and said
"I'll take this and, um, a stereo."
He gestured toward the Sears
Silvertone stereos and I chose
a boxy blue one with detachable
speakers for forty dollars.

Dad used to send me $60 a month
for food and school supplies. We got by
on *Kraft* Macaroni and Cheese Dinners,
canned soup, spaghetti with instant sauce
mix. I knew that this purchase wasn't
going to improve our menu choices.

I carried the huge boxed blue stereo
several blocks to the bus stop, took
the two buses back to Cheektowaga,
walked several blocks to the house,
carried the stereo

up the stairs to our flat,
set it up and put the album on
to play. Mickie and I listened to
that album for six months straight
until we graduated and left Buffalo.

Thirty-four years years later, we
got tickets to see Richie Havens
perform live for the first time at
R.I.T.'s Ingle Auditorium. He was
still a stellar singer-songwriter,
with unparalleled passion, his
rough rich voice cut through all
obstacles, spreading his love gospels.

After the show, he came out to meet
people, sell and autograph his new
CD's. Fans brought albums from
home for him to sign, proud of
how long they'd been his fans.

When my turn came, I got to sit
face-to-face with the masterful,
unforgettable Richie Havens.
He took and held my hand in
both of his, as I told my story
to his squirms and sighs.
We both went back in time.
As much as my finding him
meant to me, he was touched
to silence, with glistening eyes, to
hear about two broke college girls
playing the grooves right out of
Something Else Again.

No TV

For eighteen years, people
would say, "You know
that show—where so
and so..." and I
would say "No—
I don't have
a TV."

Looks of horror
came on to me.
It didn't comfort
people that I had
a fantastic stereo,
loads of albums, scads
of books. Or that I took
yoga classes, and I loved
to walk/bike/write/cook.

"You don't watch *Friends*
on Thursday nights?" my
pal Nikki once asked me.
"No," I joked, "I *have* friends
on Thursday nights."

As if I was out of food or
water, friends showed up
at my door, unannounced:
"Here," they'd say, a small
old TV filling up their arms:
"Take it." No one got that I
had no such need; it was
the seventies and 80's.

Did I miss anything?

Breaking Up Over Indian Food With a Table Between Us

He reached across the table,
    "May I?" he asked
and gently took her hand.

That physical touch might
have misled fellow diners.
They were there to give closure
to their decision to break up.

Over Palak Paneer and
Vegetable Biryani, they
confessed, explained, revealed,
sighed, confronted and reviewed.
They flirted and laughed;
they had nothing to lose.

The freedom of imminent
demise took them to
a place of intimacy,
spiraling ever deeper.

Sensing a shift, he said, "Let's
leave...go somewhere else."

Gently breaking, she whispered
    "It's probably easier here,
      though, isn't it?"
"You mean with the table between us
    keeping us apart?" he asked.
"No," she said—
"with the table between us
    holding us together."

Yesterday's News

There is a certain rhythm
on Thursday mornings—
The recycling truck
and the recycling man
come to empty blue bins
of used metal—ching, ka-ching
collect and toss the glass—
sling—ping, ka-ping,
the newspapers—flap, slap, flap —
Then—ba-boom—he tosses
the empty blue bin
back on the sidewalk,
without a glance.
But this morning I saw the recycling man
stand totally still, as a mannequin would.
He was holding a section
of recycled newspaper—
stretched out between both of his hands,
as if it was all he had to do in this world.

Rush-hour traffic was merging
around him—beep-honk—beep!
And the giant recycling
truck's engine was idling,
ready to take on the load
of glass— sling, ping,
of metal — ching, ka-ching —
He stared at the paper.

All the way, as I was driving to work,
I imagined what was engrossing to him.
Something had taken him out of
the present moment, oblivious
to all that was happening around
him. Was it the obituary (gasp)

beep, beep—"*Hey pal!*"
of an old friend?
Heartbeat—ba-boom, ba-boom—
or maybe a wedding photo—
his high school girlfriend?
Slap, flap, fla—ka-boom!
It could have been the story
about the humpback whales—
Honk, honk— "*Hey buddy—*"
the one reporting on the study
that says their singing is language
for them—how they communicate!
"*Haven't got all day, pal!*"
Ping, ka-ching . . . wow!
or maybe he noticed some
personal ad: "SWF, baggage-free,
sense of humor, seeks regular guy . . ."
"*Move it buddy!*"
"to share Abbott's custard, walks
on the pier, The Little Theater . . .LTR."

Or he could have been reading
the classified section: the perfect
hedge trimmer or a gifted pet
monkey, skilled at sorting recyclables —

I don't know *what* he was reading!
I wish I could know—
what collection of words
stopped time for this man—
and made all of the present
take a back seat.
Just for a second,
let me be in his shoes—
reading an untimely slice
of yesterday's news.

Singing the Blues

The girl is seven.
Her two brothers, slightly
older, tease and taunt
her *mercilessly*.

Their grandmother, Maryann,
tells me when one of the boys plays
piano, the girl sings her own sad words
from another room in the house.

"She sings the blues!" Maryann cries,
"She sings about the sorrows
  of a tortured life
   and love lost!"

Maryann wonders why her son's
wife doesn't protect her daughter
  from the boys.
I wonder how the child found
her gift among the ruins
  of compassion.

Linked by genes and the sand
that passed through a shared
hourglass, the kids will
find the right path.

Maybe they'll move hundred of miles
apart; their past like a gaping
canyon between them—

Or maybe they'll become
a touring band,
singing the truth—
for all to hear.

I Saw That Guy Today

I saw that guy today—
   the one we always see.
He hangs with his old cronies
like he's some Mustache Pete.

He looked like any old dope
just some guy off the street—
   not like he owns the place—
more like he's tired and beat.

The way he usually looks—
he hangs with empty suits
   as he holds court all day;
but all their points are moot.

That restaurant is hot.
   Meat eater cops drop in;
they clock around the place
and watch him count the skim.

I glanced out from my car;
   he never saw my eyes.
He stood there all alone,
   no "Mr. Big" disguise.

I could have called his bluff — I
should have snapped his photo:
   My silver bullet camera:
   I could have shot him cold!

B.B. King On Christmas Eve

"Life Ain't Nothin' But a Party,"
is the song I play when I'm
trimming my Christmas Tree.
No Christmas Carols for
me, with their "White
Christmas," heartbreak
and sadness. No, I play
  B.B. King. His song
continues: "Tomorrow
too soon is yesterday..."

There is sadness in that
song; but it's not maudlin
sadness. It slips down like
a spiked hot cider, warming
your chest, then your belly
before you even realize
  you took a sip.
It's B.B.'s giant warmth
and wonder about life.
He doesn't tell you about
the woman who left him
without telling you how
good it was to have her
in the first place.
He makes you want
to dance and cry at
  the same time
Even if
you're alone
on Christmas Eve.

Especially
if you're alone
on Christmas Eve.

Omega Poetry Workshop 2005

We arrived at Omega Institute on Sunday night,
straight from all the places we work full-time,
in various states—everything
new, everyone a stranger.

By Wednesday, a softening took place.
By then we had shared three days of
meals, around tables of eight,
shared the most challenging
days of our lives. We paused
on a sun-drenched Café deck,
nursed in the August air, sprung
for a cappuccino or snack, filled
the hourglasses of our lives
with new found sand, deep-
cleaned past perspectives,
removing painted memories
from our walls, demolished some
walls. Sapphire stoked the fires.
Fran swore — he meant to leave
us some room on his stage. He
missed our amazing *Open Mic*,
but his friends came first; and we
were making new ones to keep—
along with promises to write.
Friday, with Fran tied to a chair,
all thirty-seven of us stood up, one
at a time, stopwatch running,
bravely receptive to feedback,
while he listened, responded
with insight. In the end, he
was brilliant. We got what
we paid for, took home
our revisions, and his
passion for poetry.

Running Into "Dr. K" At the Jazz Fest

"Hey,"
"Hey." was all
they had to say
nine years after;
not another
word.

Still, *How Deep
Is The Ocean*
was the
next
live tune
she heard.

Red Cross a Point Mint

They said my irony was too low
to give blood today—rats!
Weirdly, I noticed,
driving back home,
the *windows* were all
boarded up at *Eastman Glass*.

They gave me a list
of foods to raisin my
irony...including *mo
lasses* and *chick peas*.
I thought that was
sexist, to say the least.

They always call and say
they *need my type*.
But it's easy to be *a
knee mic*; their stan
derds are so darn high,
it's hard to reach 'em.

They tell me to *beef up*
for at least a week
then make another *a
point mint* down there
at Red Cross
by Eastman Glass.

Low on irony.
That'll be the day.

Nonsense

I'm putting my eyes in my pocket
   my nose in the sky—
   don't wanna catch your cold
   when you walk by—

sneezing and crying, little
   baby on fire, jammin' so
   wrong, mama, one sock missing,
   the other shoe gone.

I sit at your work bench;
   you nail a sad song—
   you give it too much thought.
   It takes you way too long.
   we carved a pumpkin once here—
   so a candle lived on.

I'm putting words in my purse,
all my thoughts underground.
   you can't talk to me;
you better think out loud.

We're getting older on Friday
   and your cat's wearing fur
   what happened to our youth?
   there must be a cure.

Keep your dough in your rocket;
   put your head to the sky
   be sure you watch me wink
   as your band rolls by.

Badi Assad Concert/High School Graduation

Rochester Int'l Jazz Festival Tent, June, 2006

Badi takes us
to another place
a time we sense
but cannot name—
She holds back
no cry no bark
      no chirp no
wail, no past life
chant, no dance
no breakthrough:
she's giving birth
she's popping corn
she's a 5 piece-band,
she a gypsy and a
stranger,
      an exotic bird
flying into our
      lives for an
hour, into our
cagey hearts
      forever.
Behind me stand
      two extremely
      reserved men
uncomfortable
      without chairs.

Outside the Eastman Theater
youthful thunder—a sea
of long black gowns, flying
mortar boards, red confetti,
proud parents in tears.

The Missing Poem

She rejected that poem
for excessive cuteness,
Tossed it out for having
      no substance,
an empty suit.

It's unseemly to flirt
she said, with these
uptown poems, on
which she'd worked so
hard. She let it go
for its hollow tone,
fired it for its lack
of spark or flame.

No one gets in
the man-u-script
for hanging about
  like a groupie.

You must learn
to present yourself,
      to dress
for the occasion—
Consider growing up—
listen to your elders.

She made that poem
sit in detention 'til
its smirk faded
off of its face.

Bundle Of Jazz

You walked into Java's—had a satchel in your hands—
horn or violin case—I couldn't see —
You were across the room—
but then you passed by me—

"Wow!"—I exclaimed—(saw his little head of hair)
"I thought you were carrying an instrument there!"
"Well, his *name* is Jazz—" You smiled at me.
"He's two months old—actually going on three."
I let it go at first; but then I had to ask
"Why did you name him Jazz?"
You told me all these stories—(stuff
familiar to me)—about his father's
band—Jazz's Dad's history —

How the band behaves like a family — until
they break up — and then they reconvene.

When they go out to hear music, they always
groan and fret—"Can't hear the bass at all—
could you believe that set?" And all their free
time they gotta drive somewhere—
to pick up an amp, or borrow speaker wire.

"Hey," I said—"You gotta feel sorry for them!
you and me—we're the lucky ones—

We get to go out, hear some blues and jazz
nothing to haul — jes' clap our hands
digging the rhythm—
now that is a blast!"

We walk out the door
bundled up in *jazz*.

Whit Smith

Jazz Festival Tent, June 2006

Whit whips
the guitar
like he's got
a lasso in
his hand—
Django
swinging
West.
His
big
bass
walking
straight up
tent walls.

On the Way To Cedar Walton

On the way to the concert in the car
Lou said "Move over slow poke."
      (to the driver ahead of us)
I said, "There are a lot of
people here from out-of-town
this week for the Jazz Fest."

He said, "They sat through
the entire green light!" I
said, "Maybe they're getting
high." He grinned, "And I. . .
should be patient...WHY?" I said,
"You were young once, right?"

At Kilbourn Hall, Cedar Walton said
"I wanted to get my sunglasses
      off; but decided they
looked cool." I thought he
said, " 'cause they make
me look so cruel."

I like what his left hand is doing
more than his right; but clearly
      they're a pair; I can't very well
ask his left hand to play with Keith
Jarrett's right. But I'm curious
enough to consider the possibility.

I stop to wonder if Dad
would have liked *Skylark*.
      I couldn't always
guess what he'd like.
He was unpredictable
about music and cars.

Juanito Pascal

Jazz Festival, 2006

Ear honey
        eye candy
great hair
        cut from the
promo photo
Perfect
Spanish
        accent
all the stories
        still
        he hails
from
Michigan
        of all places
politely
        apologizing
for tuning,
        providing
details
        then
passionately
        playing
Flamenco
        We are
transported.

Little Jazz

Bob Sneider,
Rich Thompson,
Jeff Campbell,
Bill Dobbins.
We live here
as they do—
This is our
real Jazz Street.
Entertainment
tonight
at the Little Theater Cafe:
Independent and
foreign films,
popcorn, art,
espresso, wine,
music to open
our minds—
take the top
off our heads
make space
for all this...
Cedar could
learn from Bill
a straighter line,
a cleaner break—
a pregnant pause.
The festival has
everyone whipped
up into a frenzy,
while the cool jazz
professors from
Eastman School
give it up for free
at the end
of the week.

AAA-Scrubs-Movie

> *Oh, Lord, Won't You buy me a Mercedes Benz*
> (Janis Joplin)

Triple A guy diagnosed my *Prius*.
Said the starter battery had a dead
cell — but wouldn't tow—
said the *hybrids run*
off by themselves!

Like JD in *Scrubs*, I gazed,
envisioning my Prius being
hauled up Four Ninety East
on a flatbed truck, then
suddenly rolling off the raised
platform, grooving into
oncoming traffic to the
sound of The Cars'
      Double Trouble
no, Springsteen's *Pink Cadillac*
no, Hooker's *Mustang Sally*
no, Tracy Chapman's *Fast Car*
no, Prince's *Little Red Corvette*,
no, I've got it: The Beatles'
Baby You Can Drive My Car.

This tow truck guy talked
out of one side of his mouth.
I was still stuck inside a romantic
comedy we watched late last night,
      still sensitive to the
gas station/artist character
who almost didn't notice
his Tomboy girlfriend's
brand new red lipstick.

Toasted Crumpet Croûtons

Toasted crumpets
beg for a topping—a
cover of butter,
Nutella,
honey,
or jelly.

Turning toasted
crumpets into croûtons:
I have to
explain:
This is not England
or Wales;
I found you
in *Wegmans!*
I'm making a salad,
so in you go.

Press Conference With God

After the final darkness
      comes at last,
there will be a very
      bright light—

a spotlight on God,
surrounded by
TV cameras and
multi-media microphones,
poised steno pads,
camera bulbs flashing,
cell phones in the air,
swelled by the din of
everyone on Earth
vying for a chance
to ask in person,
the nagging, burning
questions on the
mysteries of this life...

"You made time to create
mosquitoes, Lord? And
biting black beach flies?"
"Put thorns on roses, God?"
"Four seasons...okay but...
      Flu season God?
      Tooth decay?"
"Earthquakes, tornadoes,
hurricanes—entire
summers when it rains
      only on weekends?"
You, Who are all knowing,
      all seeing, Lord,
where is Your Mercy?
You, who gave us bread,

corn, peanuts, strawberries,
avocados that melt in our
      mouths like butter,
gave us allergies to these
wonderful foods? Migraine
headaches from chocolate,
Dear God of all things? Why?

And what's the deal
with Cancer, Lord?
Breast Cancer?!!
Prostate cancer?
I thought we were supposed
to be modest and covered
after the garden and all!

Somehow I suspect, though,
seeing Him face-to-face,
there would be only
the one question:

What on earth, Lord
did we ever do to
deserve the gift of
Your sweet love?

It's Not Just the Coffee

I know you think it's a waste of money going out for coffee, Maureen; but please re-consider. It's not just high-priced coffee. It's a social life for people who work alone all day at a computer, or own a one-person business, drive a cop beat, or sit in on endless conference calls, or raise little kids.

A quiet breakfast at home with NPR can be comforting, but if you want stimulating variety in your life, find a nearby cafe and make it your clubhouse. The right coffee shop is *Cheers* minus the alcohol!

After early morning sittings at the Zen Center, we stop at *Java's* on Gibbs Street for coffee. It's an art gallery with unique music on a good sound system, excellent coffee and baked goods. Mike, the owner, brings arm loads of flowers from the public market. He buzzes around keeping the place looking inviting from morning 'til night. His beautiful barristas: Tiffany, Amber, and Mellie make us feel like family.

We've re-connected with some old pals like Jerry Laufer, a blues harmonica player and jeweler who knows and ministers to everybody. Through "The Rev" and others, we've gotten to know the policemen who stop in, other business owners. Our cousin, Bill Carpenter, might drop in with someone from the County in a suit. We love seeing my nephew Brian or other Eastman Music School students starting their day. We catch up with other musicians we know about upcoming gigs, make plans for the weekend.

Each coffee shop has a different personality. At *The Women's Coffee Connection* on South Avenue, everyone seems to come in with their best friend and not connect to anyone new. But they do great work, hiring and training women recovering from addiction, and selling Peruvian crafts, hand made by women.

Boulder Coffee, so named not for Colorado, but because there are actually boulders in the basement. No one knows how they got there. Twice cars have driven through the front of that shop! They put up a huge sign "Bruised but not Broken, " rebuilt the front, re-opened again. A great community resource in the Highland Park area, they have good music at night, art openings, a summer neighborhood festival.

It's worth visiting *Daily Perks* to see Bernie Lehman's realistic, yet magical, artwork hanging on dark orange walls. A variety of good music, easy on the eardrums, is available weekend nights at a decent hour for a small cover.

Sadly, *Patrik's Kulinary Creations* has disappeared; the tiny corner yellow building at Benton and Goodman is for rent. Too bad. The place was immaculate, the scones were hot, and Patrik has the best laugh of anyone you've ever met. Word is he moved to Washington.

At *Java's* the greetings are low key, the music is wildly unpredictable and the humor is a top priority. We get each other jump started in the morning. Sometimes we need that push — that, and the thick foam on a "skinny latte with two shots."

You better call me next time you're in town, Maureen. I'm taking you to Java's for a blueberry scone, a latte and some laughs.

Becoming the Poem

April, the whimsical painter,
introduced us at *Artisan Works*:
"Frank is a poet too!" she said.
I asked him if he goes to
Writers and Books, or to the
Open Mic's around town.
               He hesitated—
"Occasionally...maybe
      like every two years,"
he said with a wry smile.

Then, leaving intermissions
between each word, he said:
"My goal now, is to *not* write."

Amazed, I tried
      to find out why.
"So you will have time,"
      I queried
"to do something else?"
        "I hope so," he replied.

"Something in particular?"
      I prodded, (providing
suggestions, as he paused again).
        "Like painting or sculpture?"

"It's more . . that I want to . . .
. . .*become* a poem," he said.

"Ahhhh," I nodded. . . . "So you're
      through with observing,
and being the reporter."
      His wry smile widened.

You're Gone Again

You're gone again...
another plane
to catch
before sunrise
before my eyes
are re-delighted
with your smile.

On our front porch,
potted pansies brag
up their little faces
what they know of
spring and promises.

As hyacinths are deciding
which perfume to release,
you pass back yard daffodils
wearing nothing underneath
their see-through yellow costumes
heads bobbing, in garden gossip.

Forsythia stretches its long
freshly blooming stems
towards the still bare trees
above, sketching the sky.

As you glance through
 the garage window,
Buddha sees you off,
 his unconditional
peacefulness, his loyal
presence and friendship
solid as ancient stone.

About the Author

Elaine Heveron grew up in Rochester, New York where she now resides with her poet/attorney husband, Lou Faber, and one wonderful cat, Mystie. She graduated from Villa Maria College in Buffalo, NY. Her poetry is strongly influenced by her love of music, her fascination with relationships and the rhythm and blues of daily life. She has written two previous books of poetry, *Standing Room Only in My Heart* and *Sifting Through The Words*.

www.ingramcontent.com/pod-product-compliance
Lightning Source LLC
Chambersburg PA
CBHW071004080526
44587CB00015B/2338